THE

FENIAN BROTHERHOOD.

A FEW USEFUL HINTS TO IRISHMEN,
AND SOME VALUABLE INFORMATION FOR AMERICANS,
CONCERNING IRELAND.

BY AN IRISHMAN.

BOSTON:
PRESS OF DAKIN, DAVIES, & METCALF
(SUCCESSORS TO BAZIN AND CHANDLER),
NO. 37 CORNHILL.
1864.

THE

FENIAN BROTHERHOOD.

A FEW USEFUL HINTS TO IRISHMEN,
AND SOME VALUABLE INFORMATION FOR AMERICANS,
CONCERNING IRELAND.

BY AN IRISHMAN.

BOSTON:
PRESS OF DAKIN, DAVIES, & METCALF
(SUCCESSORS TO BAZIN AND CHANDLER),
NO. 87 CORNHILL.
1864.

"THE FENIAN BROTHERHOOD."

On taking up the "St. Louis Daily Union," of January 20th, 1864, I was surprised, astonished, and mortified at the spirit and tenor of an article in the editorial column, headed

"THE FENIAN BROTHERHOOD."

For several years past our readers have been apprised by such fragmentary hints as obscure advertisements of meetings in the newspapers, of the existence in this country of an Irish organization, called the "Fenian Brotherhood." Until recently, but little was known of it, save that it was exclusively Irish and patriotic in its character, and secret in its organization. A copy of the "Proceedings of the First National Convention of the Fenian Brotherhood, held at Chicago, Illinois, November, 1863," gives us some insight into its objects and designs. Portions of the proceedings of this Convention are printed in cipher, the time not having arrived when it will be prudent to make them public. Some suspicious persons have conjectured that the aims of the association were in some way inconsistent with American liberties; and others have connected with it a vague Roman Catholic Guy Fawkes gunpowder plot for blowing up Protestantism. A careful and scrutinizing examination of the resolutions of this Convention, and of the frank speeches made during its sittings, fails to bring to our observation the slight evidence of either design. The object of the Brotherhood is entirely transatlantic. It is *the rescue of Ireland, by armed force, from British rule*, and the rehabilitation, after centuries of prostration, of the ancient Irish Kingdom. Religious and political ends are totally ignored, and all natives of Ireland and children of Irish parents, who are willing to labor for the disenthralment of Ireland, are welcomed to the organization. The Brotherhood in this country was first organized at New York, in 1858, — six years ago. It now extends over the whole land, having a circle in nearly every city in the United States. The stimulus which the natural martial spirit of the Irish has received from the enlistment of so many of them in the present war, has given a marvellous impetus to the progress of the organization, and, by demonstrating the military genius of the American-Irish people, has brought more temptingly before their eyes the great object which they seem so abundantly able to achieve. The consciousness of their power to achieve it, too, makes them impatient to begin. The following resolutions, which we take from the proceedings before us, will more clearly illustrate the designs of the Brotherhood: —

1. *Resolved*, That we, the Centres and Delegates of the said Fenian Brotherhood, assembled in this our first annual Convention, do hereby emphatically proclaim our organization to consist of an association having for its object the national freedom of Ireland, and composed for the most part of citizens of the United States of America, of Irish birth or descent, but open to such other dwellers on the American continent as are friendly to the liberation of Ireland from the domination of England, by every honorable means within our reach, collectively and individually, save and except such means as may be in violation of the Constitution and laws under which we live, and to which all of us, who are citizens of the United States, owe our allegiance. We furthermore boldly and firmly assert our unquestionable right under the said Constitution and laws, to associate together for the above-named object, or for any similar one; and to assist with our money, our moral and political influence, or, if it so pleases ourselves, with our persons and our lives, in liberating any enslaved land under the sun.

2. *Resolved*, That we, the representatives of the Fenian Brotherhood in the United States, do hereby solemnly declare, without limit or reservation, our entire allegiance to the Constitution and laws of the United States of America.

Whereas, also, the thousands of well-trained Irish-American soldiers, and the officers, who are at present longing to strike for the freedom of their fatherland, will dwindle away in equal ratio, if no opportunity be given them to serve their own country, while the vigor of their manhood remains unbroken; be it

10. *Resolved*, That we call upon and exhort every true Irishman in America, England, and the British Colonies, to rally around the Fenian Brotherhood, and to aid us in preparing Ireland for freedom's battle, and in hastening the day of her deliverance; and that we, with equal fervor, exhort our brothers in Ireland to hold by our be-

loved land to the last extremity, nor flee from it to foreign countries; to gird their loins silently and sternly for the inevitable struggle that is approaching.

The following is an extract from the "Address to the People of Ireland," adopted by the Convention: —

"Here we have soldiers armed and trained (thousands of them trained in the tented field, and amid the smoke and thunders of battle), with able and experienced generals to lead them. Let the cities and towns and parishes of Ireland have their brigades, regiments, battalions, and companies of partially disciplined soldiers of liberty silently enrolled. Above all things, let every man be pledged to obey the commands of his superiors, and pledged, also, never to move without such commands; for obedience to command is the first and the most important requisite to the perfect soldier; all the rest is secondary."

These resolutions show that the English Government snuffed a real danger when it was announced, several months ago, in that country, that "an organization called the Fenian Brotherhood was contemplating a revolution in Ireland." When that revolution is begun, it will be an ugly business. A million of adult Irishmen, endowed with a physical freshness and vigor that no other people possesses; inspired by a sprightliness and tenacity of nationality that wholesale and world-wide expatriation has not been able to impair; with whom cracking crowns and breaking noses is the most fascinating of pastimes, — such a host, moved by a pervading determination to redeem their ancient land, were a spectacle that might well cause uneasiness and dismay in the Government officers of England. There may be technical informalities, and even illegalities, in the way of such a movement; but, in spite of that, a movement aiming at the regeneration of a land whose colleges were seats of learning while England was illiterate and barbaric, and whose

"Flash of wit and bright intelligence
And beam of song and blaze of eloquence"

have endeared her to the world, cannot fail of the liveliest sympathy from Americans.

The writer of the article in question seems to have regarded, at one time, this Society as rather a dangerous and unlawful organization; but upon a close acquaintance with it he seems to regard it with more favor.

Alleging that "some suspicious persons have conjectured that the aims of the association were in some way inconsistent with American liberties," and that "others have connected it with a vague Roman Catholic Guy Fawkes gunpowder plot for blowing up Protestantism." But, he says, such persons are mistaken; that "the object of the Brotherhood is entirely transatlantic. It is *the rescue of Ireland, by armed force, from British rule*"!! That is all, is it? It is certainly a very harmless occupation for American citizens to be engaged in. Just fomenting a rebellion within the limits of a power with which we are on terms of amity and friendship! That is all. A thing in no wise at variance with the duties of an American citizen; but, on the contrary, according to this writer, "cannot fail of the liveliest sympathies from Americans!"

This may be right, but I trust that *it will fail* to command the sympathy of the American people; and that erelong, such organizations will fail to command the attention, much less the sympathy, of Irishmen who have been received into the family of American citizens.

But I am loath to believe that the editors of the "Daily Union" were fully "posted" of that whereof they wrote. I am rather inclined to believe that their utter ignorance of the subject treated was the cause of such a foolish (to say the least of it) article.

The "Union," however, is not by itself in this respect. There seems to be a general impression amongst Americans that Ireland is in a dreadful condition of oppression; the British lion having hold of the poor, bleeding country with both paws, squeezing its very life out (which is fast ebbing into America), and committing all sorts of unheard-of atrocities.

Now the fitting reply to this would be (though not very classical) "bosh,"—pure, sheer, unadulterated "bosh." But when these impressions take the form of such organizations as the Fenian Brotherhood, and come recommended, by the editor of an influential American newspaper, to the sympathies of American citizens, perhaps, by way of reply, a statement of a few facts may not be out of place.

The Irish come to this country by the thousands. They are asked what makes them leave Ireland. To this they have an answer, "cut and dry,"—oppression. British oppression is the cause. They are so down-trodden that they cannot stand it any longer, and in consequence are forced to leave the land of their birth. This, or something to this effect, would be the reply from nineteen out of every twenty *Roman Catholic Irishmen* to the above question. Let us examine a few of the reasons which cause the Irish to leave Ireland, and let the facts speak for themselves.

The farmer in Ireland is one on a very small scale; the greatest number of farms being in size from three to fifteen acres. Potatoes were the chief, I might say almost the only, article of subsistence, alike for man and beast. These the farmer cultivated, by the labor of his own hands; when they failed, as in 1846, all failed; very few being able to employ any other kind of labor; and other crops could not be raised thereby exclusively to any advantage, and thus the poor farmer was left to subsist on charity, or flee from the country which had given him birth.

In this trying crisis, their only consolation and hope was in the advice of their spiritual leaders. All earthly support seemed to fail them. They became dispirited; could not raise the potatoes to "fatten the pig;" to "pay the rent" with; and landlords are there as they are here, and everywhere, quick in dispossessing a non-paying tenant. In this extremity if he has got anything left him wherewith to pay his passage out, on board an emigrant ship, with a heart like to break, he leaves the land of his fathers and seeks a home in the Western world, where his labor soon places him above the reach of want, and not unfrequently enables him to extend a helping hand to some poor relative at home, who is anxious to better his condition by selling the honest "sweat of his brow," in the best market.

Here, then, is one cause of so large an emigration of Irish to this country since 1846. It has been charged upon the British Government that, at the time here referred to, it left the poor of Ireland to die uncared for, etc. The Government appropriated twenty millions of dollars for the relief of the suffering poor, and made every disposition of the same which was calculated to save the lives of the poor, famished people. Yet notwithstanding their efforts, great suffering was endured, and many died of starvation before the aid, thus tendered, could be applied.

Another cause of the poverty which is so general in Ireland, is to be found in the land monopoly of the country. But this is not confined to Ireland, but is the cause of poverty in all of the countries of Europe where it exists, and it exists in them all.

A great deal of land in Ireland changed hands during the Cromwell period, and at other times when waging war with England, while a still greater portion remained in the hands of the old Irish chiefs, and still continues to remain in their hands to this day. The question of "Who owns the land?" is of very little importance to the poor tenant. He has to pay his rent alike to the non-resident English landowner, and the resident Irish chief.

Reforms of a very important character have been effected in this land question, of late years, by the enforcement of an Act of Parliament, entitled "The Encumbered Estates Court Act," and by which the "law of entail," and of "feudal tenures" has been practically abolished in certain cases. The writer is acquainted with men who have no titles to greatness but such as they have achieved by their own indomitable perseverance and industry, who have purchased estates, under the provisions of the above act, which were formerly owned and could be owned only by such as had inherited some high landing title, or had some conferred upon them by the gift of the Crown. The question of land monopoly is the same in Ireland as it is in either England or Scotland, or indeed any other country where feudalism ever prevailed.

But another and more direct cause of poverty in Ireland than either of the two mentioned, is to be found in the fact that, comparatively speaking, no modern manufactures have been established or introduced into that country. If we except the linen of the north, there is nothing else left to note in their manufactured exports. While England and Scotland have been vying with each other in the various walks of competitive industry, Ireland has stood aloof, and scarcely may be noted as having entered the lists. Any of those countries would be in the same condition which Ireland is in to-day, were it not for employment given to the thousands of their poor, in their cotton, woollen, and iron factories. Cast abroad upon the country the populations of London, of Liverpool, of Manchester, of Glasgow, and of the many other manufacturing towns in England and Scotland, and the consequence would be the same precisely as it is in Ireland. The land would be divided and cut up into small farms, and the great mass of the people, instead of industrious artisans, enriching themselves and their country by the products of their mechanical genius and skill, would be a horde of poor shiftless peasants, unable to do more than grow in good seasons sufficient to feed and clothe themselves and their families.

But why this? Why have manufactures not been introduced in Ireland as well as the other countries mentioned? This query will at once suggest itself. I will endeavor to answer it.

The Irish are a highly imaginative people. They are full of the poetry and eloquence of nature. The good old times of yore, with all their chivalric usages, were more congenial to the heart and feelings of an Irishman than the clatter and din of a modern mechanic's shop. Perhaps this feeling is nowhere more intense than among the upper classes in Ireland. Do you think that a veritable scion of the famous Brian the Brave would leave his wealth, or his social standing, or indeed *descend* to such things as mechanics or commerce! Nay, verily! He spends his income and his time in the glorious sport of the steeple-chase, or in giving and holding levees, endeavoring thereby to carry his mind back to past ages, from the otherwise practical scenes of the present. While English and Scotch noblemen, in the early part of the present century, encouraged and promoted by their influence and their wealth the then budding industrial Arts, which have since grown to a giant's stature, the noblemen of Ireland were either frittering away their time in the spirits of the chase, or engaging in the useless agitation of some political *ignis fatuus.* Were the political and social leaders of the Irish people to set themselves about doing good for their country, they would at once take such steps as might be necessary to establish manufactures in that country. There is every requisite necessary to place Ireland in the foremost rank as a manufacturing country. Her sons are to be found in almost every workshop of England and Scotland, and also in this country. The surface of the country is perhaps as beautifully watered and well adapted at all points for commercial purposes as any other country on the globe. Her coal and iron fields are extensive; and indeed on the whole, it is hard to find a country for which nature has done more and man less.

Such, in brief, is the sum and substance of Ireland's miseries. There is no special taxation imposed on Ireland. No special legislation for her, if we except the appropriations which are made yearly from the public purse for the education of her poor, and for the relief of the suffering poor of the country. This is all the special kind of legislation I am aware of that is made on behalf of Ireland. Yet she is down-trodden and oppressed; her people leave her because of the oppressive acts of the British Government!! You will by this time see why I told you that the fitting reply to such charges was "bosh."

Now, how do the "Fenian Brothers" expect to relieve the miseries of their mother country? By cutting asunder the bonds of connection with England and Scotland? I cannot see, and I think the impartial reader will fail to see, how that would better the condition of the country. Do they propose to abolish, without regard to right, the system of "feudal tenures," dividing the land out among the tenantry of the respective estates? This would really do no good, if it could be accomplished peacefully; but when attended, as it most undoubtedly would be, by the shedding of brothers' blood, if for no other cause, it ought not to be attempted.

They know not what they are aiming at. The government of Great Britain is a free Protestant government. She has established free secular schools in Ireland, in which religion of any kind is not permitted to be taught; and on this account, more than any other, is she detested, and hated by the Irish Catholic clergy. In this particular, they went so far as to, in some instances, excommunicate parents who sent their children to these schools. If there is any oppression, it is the oppression of the priest, which is the worst oppression of all.

Fellow countrymen, take the words of solemn warning and advice, which I see thrown out to *you* occasionally from that sagacious statesman, eloquent orator, and patriotic countryman, Thomas D'Arcy McGee. He has seen his follies and his blunders, and like an honest man and true patriot points out the snares that are laid for you by a few designing demagogues and disappointed politicians.

Remember, also, your duties as American citizens. You are plotting mischief and hostility to a power with which the government of the United States is at peace.

The government of Great Britain has forbidden, and has seized without authority of local law, armed vessels, when they were fairly and fully satisfied that said vessels were to be employed in hostility to the government of this country. She has more recently given us intimation of plots and schemes of rebel agitators and disaffected citizens of the United States going on within her borders; and shall it be said in the face of this conduct, that Irishmen will go on with their foolish and mischievous schemes of hostility to that same government? Do you desire a separate and independent form of government for Ireland, as a remedy for the evils complained of? Most assuredly that would only aggravate them. The interest of those three kingdoms is so interwoven with each other, that to talk of a separate and independent form of government for either of them, is only to talk absurdity and foolishness, with a view to practise both. Aim to understand your true position. You came to this country for the very same reasons which take thousands of American-born citizens from the Eastern States out to the great West, — to make money, and to better their condition generally. You do the same. Labor is better paid here than it is in Ireland; but still the wealthy lord it over the poor here as well as there. There are no laws in either country which in any way interfere with society in this respect. Priests are unwilling that you should be educated unless they can have charge of your education; hence the bitterness of that feeling which exists among them, as a body, to the British Government. They are even averse to the introduction of those practical arts among you which necessitate men to *think*. They would rather that you would all live in poverty and ignorance than that you should become enlightened, wealthy, and rational in religious matters.

If you desire to do some good for your mother country, enter into associations for the establishment of manufactures of every kind. Then will the poor of the country find profitable employment without having to quit their homes. Then will populous and wealthy cities spring up, and the art of man will then be found in sweet alliance with nature, embellishing that "gem of the sea." Then will the poor ignorant peasant, who can scarcely eke out a bare livelihood for himself and family, merge into the more exalted sphere of the intelligent and industrious artisan, enriching himself and his country by the products of his mechanical skill. Let your means and your energies be employed in this way, and much practical good will result therefrom.

But what can result from such foolish enterprises as that of the "Fenian Brotherhood"? You only beget the ridicule of the world, and the contempt of those whom you esteem as enemies.

I trust yet to see more prosperous days for the country which gave me birth; but from the knowledge which I have of her people, and her resources, of her situation geographically, and of her relations socially with England and Scotland, I can only look for that prosperity to come by the application of the means indicated.

MAC.

www.ingramcontent.com/pod-product-compliance
Lightning Source LLC
LaVergne TN
LVHW020644110826
845149LV00004B/1351

* 9 7 8 1 4 1 8 1 8 9 9 3 8 *